Beyond the Shallows

PUBLISHED BY
MISSION POSSIBLE PEOPLE
1066 New Beginnings Ln.
Clifton, TN 38425

www.MissionPossiblePeople.com

ISBN: 978-0-9960465-4-1

First Printing 2021

Cover & interior design by Nelly Murariu at PixBeeDesign.com

Beyond the Shallows

*Poetic insights to inspire,
reflect upon and enjoy*

KENNEDY BROWN

To my wife
Janelle Wiseman Brown

"Why?" you might ask.

Let me quote, in her own words, her encouraging response to my Facebook post of a poem:

"Dear husband, you simply amaze me. Most of our married years you never wrote much more than postcards and checks! But I saw you write the poem 'True North' in less than an hour! I'm so glad God gifted you in being a poet, and I didn't even know it."

TABLE OF CONTENTS

PREFACE

Throughout my life I had consistently waded in the shallows of deep thinking. Then, on December 15, 2015, the midpoint of my 85th year—miracle of miracles—God's spirit interrupted my spirit with a burst of verse. Although a tentative step into deeper spiritual waters, my first poem was a hesitant, fitful start. The initial burst continued to flow, taking on many different rhyming and non rhyming styles—resulting in the following eclectic collection of style and theme. The verse ranges from deeper spiritual insight to haiku tomfoolery.

Let me adjure you, please ignore the lack of descriptive caress which the right brained poet might have offered. Instead, just read, pondering where called for and laughing when inspired.

Kennedy Brown
Gerizim* (January 13, 2017)

*Gerizim is the name we gave our home in the hills of
western Tennessee. See Deuteronomy 11:29.

INTRODUCTION

Beyond the shallows
Into the depths of His Love
Life's great adventure

BEYOND THE SHALLOWS

I no longer stay in the shallow waters of our relationship, where I built sand castles life's tides dissolved.

I now voyage out into the deep, secure in the vessel He has crafted for me.

As I plumb these new depths, the excitement returns that as a child I first experienced in the tide pools left by the retreating waves.

For too long I was content in our relationship, my grown body an exaggeration in those safe waters.

Even though I am now old and gray, He beckons me to trust, to experience, to revitalize.

And so I have left the benign safety of the shallows—reaching to grasp His outstretched hand, being lifted aboard the vessel Discovery, sailing toward Intimacy—sails filled with His Spirit's wind.

CHAPTER ONE

Where it all began

Bald head, shaggy beard—
What eighty-six years hath wrought.
Anticipation

A PSALM FROM A BRIDE

A CONSIDERATION OF REVELATION 19:7-8 AND 22:17

A psalm I write, O Yeshua, with cadence ordered—
My soul's words of measured stride—
Ascending for Your eternal awareness—
To my Bridegroom from His bride.

But how do I approach with this masculine frame?
How can I seek Your face, Your embrace?
My soul knows only the calloused hand—
My soul knows only to love as a man.

Not my soul, my spirit must give the count—
Not a march, a flight to heaven's realm—
Finding succor at Abba's breast—
To ever guide my questioning soul.

My psalm, dear Yeshua, no longer strident.
This bride knows no gender—
My spirit at rest in God's presence
Delighting in Love's eternal embrace.

Motivation for poem—

This poem comes first, because it was first. It was the spiritual download that began my "poetic phase."

As I was reading Psalm 17 in Don Esposito's bible translation *Hebraic Roots Bible,* I felt an inspiration to write a psalm.

The words just seemed to flow as I attempted to articulate in somewhat psalmist format the desire to worship as a bride, Yeshua, my Bridegroom. The effort progressed and I soon realized that only as my human spirit understood could my soul (mind and emotions) understand. My human spirit acted as a nexus-interpreter between Yahweh's Spirit and my soul. This has continued to be the "mental block breaker" as I give poetic expression to ongoing impressions.

December 18, 2015

FEVERED POETIC

Once from fever's leaven I wrote with poetic meter.
The words flowed with heated inspiration—
Making bright the darkest night—
My pen spewed forth great deeds of valor.

With lance and shield and in armor clad
I was poetically more than equal to mythical Galahad.
Yet, from the fevered brain's cool recesses
In crept reality to staunch my ink's flow—

My sick-bed held me with vengeful grasp—
Lance fell, it could strike no blow—
And shield too slid toward the ground.
Nothing left but fevered gasp:

"Galahad, to you I bend my knee."
Fiction has won over life's reality.

Motivation for poem—

As I walked from the house down to the barn today I recalled 65 years earlier when the Poet's inspiration briefly visited me. It was toward the end of my six-week ROTC summer camp in Ft Hood, Texas.

I didn't know it at the time, but my body was fighting what would later be diagnosed as TB. Needless to say, Ft Hood in July in a Sherman tank is a very hot place. This heat accelerated the fever I must have been running. I didn't go on sick call as the "whiners" were doing. I was a DMS (Distinguished Military Student). For me such weakness would have been "conduct unbecoming a future officer."

During this stressful time I wrote long, epic poems of love and valor. Unfortunately, or maybe fortunately, I didn't save any of them. It is interesting, however, how the fevered brain can churn out reams of poetic verbiage. I wonder if there are certain creative chemical connections made in the brain as a result of stress?

I am humbled and thankful that Poetry found me again. And, that my relationship with Yahweh through Yeshua allowed my renewed spirit to make creative, poetic connections from a place of health, not sickness.

March 21, 2016

A PSALM ABOUT A LOST PSALM

Yahweh, a psalm I was writing is lost.
I fear it's been cyber-space tossed.
And now I get my pride to measure—
For whom was I writing the poetic treasure?

I lament and search for the words now gone—
As snow from a springtime lawn.
True, it's the sun that aids this fact—
Perhaps then another is in this klepto act.

Wash my heart from author's pride.
Let me go forth in innocent stride.
I pray those words to You previously penned
Can now reflect love washed from sin.

As You once told me when a data crash—
You still knew every word—none were ash.

Motivation for poem—

How often have you worked on an electronic project only to have it lost? My biggest frustrations have come in the realm of computers. I am of a generation that is almost out of step with these electronic marvels. I do have an iPad, iPhone and a desktop iMac, but there is a substantial difference between owning and confidently using these wonderful devices.

As the poem makes reference, one of my most memorable meltdowns came years ago with a Bible software program. I had numerous notes and cross references catalogued—all significant, personal insights. I received an update from the software vendor. No problem—jumped right on it. Then I discovered all of my precious information was gone! The software update had neglected to mention any need to backup the data before installing the update.

The momentary comfort of hope that somehow I might be able to retrieve my lost data soon gave way to utter despair. I had a real melt down. Overwhelmed by this unresolvable, internal mental conflict, I jumped up from my desk and began the most earnest praying I can remember. As a consequence, I felt the Lord assure me He still had full knowledge of my precious information and would give me recall as I had need.

A Psalm about a Lost Psalm was a near repeat of that first meltdown experience, but this time with healing introspection.

Erev Shabbat, February 12, 2016

TRAUMA DELETE
FOR TV NEWS

Never have I ventured to express such plight
As oft strikes me by day's last light.
Before the luminous screen I sit—my legs are loosely crossed
From that screen—the daily news—is being so artfully tossed.

And then before I hardly know
My eyes have drooped—the news drones on—
Were it not for supper's call, I may sleep 'til dawn.

This is time spent without reward
As my numbed senses still record
The reported murders, robberies and vehicle wrecks.
Yet, I wait 'til ten o'clock to hear again each sordid tale
Of lust and death and those bound for jail.

At last comes that awaited final story
The uplifting one about widow, child or dog
Told to delete those reports from sin's primordial bog.
This one act of goodness is presented to erase
The emotional trauma of evil—leaving not a trace.

Is my head now ready for a good night's sleep?
Surely into it remnants of the evening news will creep.
Fortunately, for those spiritually equipped—
Prayer closes doors—Satan's plans are nipped.

Motivation for poem—

While on the theme of frustration, I'll submit another area of angst. This poem sets it forth.

I often find I doze as I sit before the tube, as the TV was once called, watching the evening news. We know that our subconscious continues to record, even when the conscious is unconscious.

My wife casually suggested that I not watch the news, thereby eliminating my tube viewing trauma. But I stay informed of current events with my evening news ritual. It's my small talk fodder for friends and family. Not to mention it's the way I unwind at the end of the day. However, I'm not completely disagreeing with my wife's "sensible" solution. I do know I must give myself some bit of emotional restoration before phosphorescent fatigue takes over at the end of the day.

I have established my own cleansing practice. After turning off the light at night, and before sleep sets in, I pray a personalized version of Psalm 91. Even though I don't specifically negate the news, I embrace all of Father's promises for protection and care—my trauma delete button, if you will. My current events conversations are still intact and so is my heart. I now sleep remarkably well.

CHAPTER TWO

Psalms from my human spirit to my soul

When first I began
It was from unction's demand—
Spirit to spirit.

A LAMENT FOR BEZALEL, CHOSEN OF YAHWEH

PARSHAT VAYAKHEL, ESPECIALLY EXODUS 35:30-35

Bezalel, O Bezalel, you by Yahweh commended
To craft the earthly work of holy inspiration—
Chosen alone from all the Hebrew nation
Upon you the Spirit of God descended.

That you were a young man, it is surmised,
Yet with the jeweler's skill and the engraver's hand
The tabernacle was soon raised upon the desert's sand.
Everyone except Yahweh was surprised.

Bezalel, anointed by Yahweh in Sinai land,
Tell us, now, what is your great reward?
You surely fell as though slain by sword;
Your bones remain in the desert's sand.

Was it the spies' report which you heeded—
Or your lust for a Midianite maiden fair?
What fatal sin will your eternal records bare?
Is there not a lesson Yahweh's children needed?

A lament, O Bezalel, I now humbly offer:
Though my giftings flow from God's own hand,
I too may find my bones in desert sand.

Motivation for poem—

While reading the Torah portion, *Vayakhel* (Exodus 35:1-38:20), I was impressed how Yahweh's favor resulted in the young man Bezalel being called and equipped for the construction of the desert tabernacle.

Rabbi David Fohrman (AlephBeta.org) explained that the past tense form of the Hebrew words used to describe God's equipping of Bezalel would indicate that He had in mind Bezalel and His plans for the tabernacle from the beginning of Creation.

But then I realized that even with this anointing and favor, Bezalel did not enter into the promised land. He died with his generation in the desert wilderness.

This man, who was called and equipped by God for the construction of the Tabernacle, missed the final reward. I don't want to live merely without losing my salvation. Rather I want salvation and my reward! His sobering tale called me to personal introspection.

I trust the "lament" captures this reality.

Erev Shabbat, March 4, 2016

A PSALM FROM A CHOSEN ONE

PROMPTED BY EXODUS 12, DEUTERONOMY 7:6
AND JEREMIAH 3:18

Of the second exodus many have spoken
The last travail of those You have chosen.
A repeat, it has been said,
Of the flight first begun with unleavened bread.

Forever marked by annual remembrance
Of blood placed on the door's jamb and lintel.
Not just any blood would do
It must be that of a lamb most true.

Was not this shed blood, dear Father
A foretelling of Messiah's own ardor?
Yourself come to sacrifice mortal flesh
That I might have my life renewed—made fresh.

And so, I too joined those blood bought ranks
Chosen forever—my eternal thanks.
Should I be on that final journey of which I spoke
Let me not be daunted at Your fire and smoke.

As I travel with those of Your chosen train
Walking the path to millennial reign—
I pray unbelief not cause me to stumble;
That I take no Sinai faint-hearted tumble.

Bones of Your chosen, who from Egypt fled,
Lay short of the Promised Land quite dead.
Yahovah, let me remember what I learn—
Your commandments and Torah never to spurn.

Motivation for poem—

Certainly parsha (portion) *Bo* (Ex 10:1-13:6) was the foundation for much of this psalm. However, the whole of Yahweh's plan, from Creation to Completion, had to be touched upon to express my prayer and praise.

I continue to be cautioned by the fact the generation leaving Egypt did not enter the promised land. Then there is the question of the second or greater exodus: Jeremiah and other prophets seem to establish that some event similar to the first exodus will occur. Perhaps this will be the period of tribulation ending in the millennial reign of Yeshua.

To remain faithful to the entire word of Yahweh, I'm convinced, will equip me to face the twists and turns of the journey, whether or not I correctly discern them now. This, of course, is possible only because of my Blood-bought relationship with Father purchased for me by Yeshua.

Sabbath, January 16, 2016

PSALM FROM A CLOSED HEART

AN APPLICATION OF MATTHEW 25:40.

Yahovah, let me not close my heart to another–
Let not even a small part slide from under Your cover.
When my emotions and flesh against love combine,
My heart and Yours can no longer entwine.

Cool looks and heated replies–
Uncover what I sought to disguise.
My smile, so carefully, deceitfully crafted–
Belies a heart closed–any fellowship shafted.

Must I be right in this strained relation–
Why can't I just hear Your Word–I am Your creation:
"As you do to the least of these–
You do likewise to Me whom you seek to please."

Why then do I wonder at Heaven's brass–
When my prayers lay dead as winter's grass?
You have spoken–if I could but hear,
And open my heart again, now without fear.

My closed heart goes far beyond this situation—
It seals the gates to all heavenly invitation.
You leave it to me to open my heart's closing—
The lost pathway to God's ear again exposing.

Motivation for poem—

I know the negative results of a closed heart, and yet I continue to commit this transgression as if I don't. When I notice my heart closing in order to self-protect, it requires an intentional act of my will to maintain its openness.

The unfortunate consequence of not taking a stand against the temporary comfort of self-protection is often times deterrent enough not to choose a closed heart. When I have shut down my spirit to another, I also shut down my spirit to my Heavenly Father.

Some twenty years ago the Lord used Matthew 25:40 to teach my wife, Janelle, a powerful lesson: when we close our heart to each other, we also close it to God. The verse states, "As you did it to one of the least of these, My brethren, you did it to Me." Both of us have appropriated the truth of this message, and the authenticity of our marriage relationship has greatly benefited.

I can't emphasize it enough—it requires a determined exercise of the will to open a heart once it begins to close.

January 4, 2016

A PSALM OF AFFIRMATION THROUGH THE AGES

*PROMPTED BY PARSHAT BESHALACH (EXODUS 13:17-17:16);
PSALM 118:14; ISAIAH 12:2 AND REVELATION 19:1*

"The Lord is my strength and song,
And He has become my salvation" (Exodus 15:2)

Many have said, including the sages,
These two verses transcend the ages.
Israel first spoke them when Sinai bound
Having crossed the sea on bone-dry ground.

Spoken again from King David's pen
As praises to Yahovah did ascend.
Troubles and enemies beset this man
But Yahovah's salvation was ever at hand.

Isaiah proclaimed the truth enduring—
From Mount Zion—*salvation*—again most stirring.
It was of Messiah Yeshua foretelling
In righteous words most compelling.

One last time, Revelation relates,
Heaven's multitude, the Word states,
Shouts, salvation, glory, honor and power—
The Witnesses' mantra in Babylon's last hour.

Motivation for poem—

With each Torah Parshat I listen to hear if I am being moved to find expression in writing a psalm. I am often helped by the commentary of others.

This psalm was prompted by Messianic Rabbi Russell Resnik from his book *Gateway to Torah.* His insights offer rich appreciation for each Torah portion.

It has been said that regardless of how many times you experience a Torah Parshat there is always new understanding, revelation and appreciation. In the few years I have been engaged in mining the riches of Yahovah's word, the vein of gold only broadens.

Sabbath, January 23, 2016

A PSALM OF SABBATH THANKS

Written with the wonderful revelation of the blessing of Sabbath which begins Friday at sundown with the lighting of two candles.

Two small lights are kindled as darkness descends—
Your ancient promise of rest begins.
Cares from my soul will be dispelled—
As light pierces darkness—six days' labor quelled.

Your seventh day—not hardship meant—
Not a burden—no, a holy sacrament.
Created by love—this commanded celebration
Sets man apart from all of creation.

Yeshua, Your Son, confirmed the plan—
The day was ordained for the good of man.
Before man was vexed by Satan's deceit—
This day for rest was eternally complete.

Those two small lights hold such promise
No longer am I a doubting Thomas.
With thanksgiving I now joyfully enter,
Knowing rest will follow as I keep Sabbath center.

Motivation for poem—

A major milestone in my Christian walk was when my wife and I embraced a true seventh day Sabbath on Saturday. In Hebrew it is called *Shabbat.* I have come to know the celebration and enjoyment of Shabbat, a day that has changed my relationship with Father, Abba, Yahweh and with Yeshua, Messiah!

In my book, *Exiting the Sunday Church,* I share at length the evolution of my coming into the understanding of the need and blessing that comes from observing this day of rest.

I won't endeavor to justify or defend my position here as I feel it would distract from the simplicity of the poem's ability to express Yahweh's wonderful provision as I obey His admonition to Sabbath rest.

I will, however, briefly speak to the "two candles." The use of the candle itself is a Sabbath custom. One candle represents the first Sabbath at Creation. The second candle reminds us of the Sabbath rest ordained at Mt. Sinai in the fourth of the Ten Commandments.

Shabbat, December 19, 2015

A PSALM OF THE FIRSTBORN

PROMPTED BY PARSHAT BO FROM EXODUS 13:2

*"...Consecrate to Me all the firstborn, whatever
opens the womb among the children of Israel,
both of man and beast; it is Mine."*

These words were not written to rhyme,
But their truth truly transcends time.
It is the "firstborn" that they identify
As one who would carry Yahweh's mantle high.

Be he first or second or eleventh born—
As was Joseph, who endured his brothers' scorn.
Yet, how very blessed is that man
Whose every descendant from his clan
Embraces Father's eternal plan.

There need not be just one so set apart
Who alone walks with Godly heart.
Yeshua's blood lets each proclaim
To be firstborn, whose heart is set aflame.

Birth order truly does not firstborn determine
Whether by law or spoken in sermon.
It's from a heart of Godly ardor
That one is firstborn to the Father.

Motivation for poem—

The firstborn symbolizes the vitality of a clan or a nation, even a herd or flock. For the firstborn of Egypt to be taken at the Passover was not only an emotional devastation of loss but also represents the loss of the strength of a people.

For Yahweh to require that the Israelites' firstborn be set apart to Him is not a punishment, but rather the jealous perpetuation of the plan for His earthly kingdom.

It is significant that Yahweh later substituted the entire priestly tribe of Levi for the firstborn of the other tribes. Since creation, He has conferred the honor of firstborn to each who would follow Him with consecration and dedication. In effect the entire tribe of Levi became a tribe of first born. Their service to Yahweh is established by their birth into the tribe of Levi.

My psalm celebrates being firstborn, that is, accepting and embracing the set-apart pursuit of Father. As believers in Messiah Yeshua we are to be kings and priests to His God and Father. (Rev 1:5-6)

Blessed is the man, as I am blessed, when each child, regardless of birth order, pursues the perpetuation of the eternal plans of Yahweh.

January 16, 2016

HIDDEN PROVISION RELEASED

INSPIRED BY LIFE EXPERIENCE AND CONFIRMED BY PROVERBS 3:5

There is a power deep within the soul of every man.
There is a praise written by God's own hand.
Both are released when stirred by life event—
When desperate supplication is heaven-sent.

How will this revelation from Yahweh start
To illuminate what's hidden within the heart?
Yeshua, Savior, by my sin to me concealed—
A light in the darkness—waits to be revealed.

Life's desperation—my sufficiency fully spent—
I hear now that voice released, unbent,
From my heart's depth, denied no longer,
His provision accepted, makes me stronger.

Praise you, Yahweh, Your provision seemingly hid—
Awaiting life's stress to spring open the lid;
Revealing Your Son's unchallenged power—
Equipping me—the enemy's plans to devour.

My strength of pride clothed in manly vigor,
Was never sufficient to meet life's rigor.
My heart's secret now wondrously revealed,
I embrace life's challenge—ungodly pride healed.

Motivation for poem—

After many years of enjoying success in business, I came to a situation in which I was failing. The failure involved not only my business expertise, but also my health. This event happened several years after my born again experience.

The Lord explained my success in business before being born again was simply due to the fact that He "loved me while I was yet a sinner." Now, here I was—a redeemed sinner, but failing.

To end this streak of failure, I began repenting of every sin or near sin I could think of. I even began repenting for running the stop signal's yellow light just in case that would help. It was His sovereign word again that corrected me: "You have not trusted Me, but you have leaned to your own understanding—your pride!"

Heartfelt repentance followed, and success eventually followed that. But the lesson would be repeated many more times as the truth would fade with new endeavors. My prayer is still to not be prideful in my strength. The strength of Yeshua who lives in me must be my praise.

January 8, 2016

A PSALM PROVOKED
BY EXODUS 6:9

FROM PARSHAT VA'EIRA (EXODUS 6:2-9:35)

When anguish of spirit closes my ear,
And focus on my bondage will not let me hear—
Then, dear Father, as in days of old,
Send me a man whose message is bold.

Though I might cower in self piteous fashion
Let your herald speak with heartfelt passion.
Sounding forth in terms most certain
Your promise to raise my life's dark curtain.

Speaking not only words of great power,
Let Your signs and wonders also shower.
In big and small ways let me see
My Father at work to set me free.

Oh, yes, that man that I did mention
I speak to the whole of Your invention:
Male and female You lovingly created—
Through either Your message may be related.

In Moses and Miriam, in Mordecai and Esther
Your message comes forth without sequester.
And so with Kennedy and with Janelle,
As with Dick and Jane as well.

And the anguish of which I spoke—
Was that cruel bondage life's sick joke?
Was it the consequence of sin I was reaping—
A fertile ground where conviction could start creeping?

What my mind could not hear
Another's voice helped make clear.
My spirit's hearing was restored and guided
By the "prophet" You so lovingly provided.

Motivation for poem—

"...but they did not hear Moses, because of anguish of spirit and cruel bondage." These words jumped out to me as I read the parshat passages in Exodus 6.

My wife, Janelle, has written extensively on the personal human spirit and its capacity for emotion or lack of emotion.

Clearly the years of bondage in Egypt, the sense of abandonment and the futility of their plight would have dulled the ability of the human spirit of each of the Israelites. Individually and collectively they could no longer hear the words of hope and promise being shared by Yahweh's prophet, Moses.

Whether His words come through male or female "prophet"—may I see His love in every situation of life.

A PSALM TO THE BRIDEGROOM

FROM CREATION TO THE MARRIAGE SUPPER OF THE LAMB

When did the courtship really begin?
Was it at Creation, even before sin?
Was it after the flood's great rampage—
Certainly marking the end of an age?

Was it with Abraham, Isaac or Jacob made known?
Your wooing of them was clearly shown.
It wasn't with candy, with flowers or like token—
It was first by Your surrogate so deftly spoken.

A mighty suitor You had more than proven
With ten plagues Egypt's cruel bonds were broken.
With showering of manna and parting of water
You provided bread and gave Pharaoh no quarter.

And then before Sinai's craggy splendor
Through Moses You inquire Your intended's ardor.
Israel, gathered round by ordered tribe,
To Your words each will solemnly subscribe.

Receiving the report in joyful celebration
You prepare to visit the chosen nation:
Thunder, lightning and cloud most dense—
Shofar blasts in decibels intense.

Sudden fear invades those gathered.
At Your voice, now in first person—
resolve is shattered.
To Moses they turn with their ardor fleeting—
"You hear for us—no more of this first person meeting."

And so, though chosen, they reject that embrace—
The desire of Yahweh did not take place.
He gives them the Torah and a Tabernacle plan—
Intimacy now through a priest, a middleman.

Thank You, Yahweh, for the prophets' foretelling
Of You coming in flesh—blood shed—sin quelling.
Yeshua, Messiah, Yourself manifest
Now indwell my heart—answering my quest.

And so that covenant at Sinai first spoken
Because of Yeshua no longer stands broken.
And soon Your voice will again invite—
The Indwelt Bride rising, responding with delight.

Motivation for poem—

There may be some theological questions stirred up by this poem. The premise is not that the Bridegroom was "created" with God manifesting in the flesh as His Son, Yeshua. Rather, that the wooing from the Bridegroom has been the constant theme from creation.

The poem charts some of the more manifest evidences of the Bridegroom's wooing and the frustration with "the Bride." Resolved finally with the Bridegroom returning for His Bride.

A CALL TO EMBRACE YAHWEH'S WORD

PROMPTED BY EXODUS 21:1-24:18—PARSHAT MISHPATIM (LAWS)

Yahweh, why are we so bent
On overlooking Your intent?
Your *mishpatim* first powerfully spoken
Are today disdained and recklessly broken.

Some thirty-five hundred years ago
Your radical words set the world aglow.
They became the foundation of Common Law
From which all Englishmen sought to draw.

Most every statute today can trace
Its evolution to Sinai's time and place.
But as Yeshua said, "Look to more than form—
"Let your spirit see the 'Yahweh norm.'"

Master and servant rules still apply
To every worker under Your sky—
The tools supplied by the Master remain
When the worker departs, not returning again.

Sorry to report, though, today, dear Father,
Six years of service seems of little bother.
Your Laws, which perhaps appear arcane,
Should be considered and honored again.

If the heart of each commandment we were to embrace
Our old earth might well be a heavenly place.

Motivation for poem—

For many years I walked with little regard for the instruction and commandments of Torah. Even with a knowledge of the scriptural origin found in the laws of the United States and the United Kingdom, I could not appreciate the wisdom Moses recorded under Yahweh's unction those 3500 years ago. How many times had I interpreted Yeshua's expansion of a Torah principle as *an amendment* and therefore a criticism of Torah. I now realize Yeshua, the Living Word, was shedding light on how to interpret the law. "Father, forgive me. I have been denying myself Yeshua's light by which to conduct all of life's relationships."

The poetic form I chose for this psalm forced constraints on my ability to fully develop and express my thoughts regarding today's laws on the master-servant relationship. The spirit of these laws is drawn from Torah and judicially established over centuries as the Common Law of England and of the United States. Although most of the Common Law has been codified, when there is no statute covering a particular legal question, the Common Law prevails.

I have very loosely described the law expressed in Exodus 21:1-6 concerning the Hebrew servant. The rule today states that the tools provided for an employee's work do not become his when he leaves his employment. The Torah principle, however, is much more generous. It recognizes that six years of faithful service earns a servant the right to own these tools. I was certainly never that generous as an employer.

CHAPTER THREE

A collection of poems defined by use of the word "eclectic"

Eclectic—nice word.
Many streams make the river.
Life can flow from each.

CAMO

I was in full camo
So I couldn't be seen.
The tree likewise wearing
Various shades of green.

My stealthy approach
Didn't fool tree a bit—
Stood its ground even knowing
'twould soon be hit.

Five miles an hour—
A miserly speed—
Still impact gravely wounded
My automotive steed.

The moral of the story—
Do not rely—
Full camo won't help—
Another full camo to spy.

Motivation for poem—

Decked out in camo, one morning, I set off down my steep driveway—proceeding slowly and cautiously—excited for a little morning hunt. Unfortunately, toward the bottom of the drive there is a big cherry tree at which I make a left turn to head toward the sheep shed. I wanted to feed the sheep before hunting.

As I approached the left turn my eye caught the sheep just off on my left. Momentarily, diverting my gaze to appraise the sheep's condition, drifted left and I hit the tree—thus this poem.

CELEBRATING A GRANDSON'S 18TH BIRTHDAY

When your new born eyes first saw light
And cries erupted from your tiny throat—
When mother's succor was all you sought
And sleep laid claim to many an hour—

Along with mother and with father
Two other observers also have watched.
Two others praise God for what they've seen.
Two others now give thanks.

Eighteen years have so quickly passed
And again you are now thrust forth into new light.
This time with 24 times' more incubation—
You stand lovingly prepared for life's next revelation.

Those two others—now with many, many more—
Stand cheering you on in your new adventure.
Even though this well-worn word of expression,
These two others add their sincere Congratulation!

Love and prayer for continued success,
Grandma and Grandpa

Motivation for poem—

It is somewhat obvious that this poem is prompted by the 18th birthday of a grandson. This event also coincides with high school graduation. These are two epochal events in today's society.

In the South graduation is grandly celebrated. In most U.S. schools, the 18th birthday often coincides with high school graduation. It is a watershed between mother's table and the college cafeteria. Many of life's choices will soon be presented after this second "incubation."

Speaking of incubation, why did I choose '24' as the times' multiplier for the second incubation? Seems obvious to me—the first incubation was 9 months. The second incubation is 18 years. So multiply 18 by 12 months divided by 9 months. The answer is 24. "Oh, Granddad," a befuddled grandson mused, "I never would have gotten that!" Well, that response does this granddad's heart good. I believe he could have figured it out. However, it might have taken some time and creative thinking.

As to "life's choices" that will be presented in this next phase, the foundation of 18 years has been laid. We never think it is sufficient. In our strength, as parents and grandparents, it isn't. The need for trust and reliance on Father's all-sufficiency will never cease.

April 16, 2016

THE POEM IN SONG

I love to write poems—
Some have a rhyming scheme,
Some of blank verse,
Some long, others terse.

Haiku too has found a place.
Sometimes though quite forced.
The 5-7-5 syllable race—
This inscrutable rule one must embrace

The song—way more skill needed.
Two warring factors—melody and message
Each vying for listener's pleasure—
Well written, both become the treasure

While a song at its very heart does motivate,
Embroidered by base and treble note,
Will open the senses to a higher state—
A level of ecstasy some will rate.

But humbled by lack of musical skill,
I will write no melody to invigorate.
Instead I must create in one dimension
With only syllabic tools for my invention.

Motivation for poem—

After a weekend visit from our talented son-in-law, who writes both words and music, I was struck by the poetry of song.

At the same time I realized the talent leap required to go from written poetry to poetry set to melody. Such a gifting is a lovely provision of the Lord. He has indeed given a variety of gifts.

Apostle Paul said it was all right to "desire earnestly to prophesy" (I Cor 14:39). Perhaps then it is OK for me to desire earnestly to be able to write verse set to music. With my "tin ear" that would be a miracle! Better yet, perhaps some day, I could experience a collusion of gifts—my poetry set to melody by my son-in-law. Now that would be magical!

November 6, 2016

THE MOUSE

The mouse is dead,
Deserved what befell his head.

With effrontery he ate
From my herbal sprouting plate.

Tender sprouts of Swiss chard—
Eaten with utter disregard.

Even arugula didn't survive
This rodent's destructive drive.

Finally, the fiendish appetite
Was quelled and brought quite right.

The peanut butter he could not resist.
The trap's spring fell—a heavy fist.

With justice rendered—
The mouse is dead.

Motivation for poem—

I transplanted the sprouted Swiss chard and arugula into pots and put the pots in a wagon. This way I could move them in and out of the garage daily to avoid freezing weather.

One morning I went to put them out and noticed the tops were almost all eaten off. What could have done it?

My wife asked if I had sprayed them for insects. I thought it too late in the season for such pests, and couldn't imagine that insects were the problem—but what else could it be?!

Finally, I set a trap in one of the pots baited with peanut butter and next morning found, quite dead, the party I assume was guilty of my plants' decapitation.

December 4, 2016

A SISTER MISSED

Now as I peer back over my slowly fading yesteryears
Seeking to recall faces and names of friends and relations
Most have passed—becoming hazy recollections,
But one remains as vibrant as today.

Small, sweet vignettes of times together
Crowd to the front when thoughts touch that one.
My first ten years were without knowledge such would be...
Then for the seventy years following I was rewarded by devoted
    sibling affection.

What a surprise that from shared roots
Can be born and bonded such a cherished, close relation.
Our age difference could have made us incompatible—
But for me, older, big brother—a role near to "proud parent,"

Flooded memories of her every age and achievement come—
From farm life to teen-year dance lessons to wife to mother and then
    to grandmother hood.
And shining through every recalled event—her overriding, radiant smile,
An infectious laugh, an unrelenting love for family and friends.
Oh yes, that fading past of which I first spoke—she too was:
The family chronicler, the confidante of aunts and uncles,
The link between cousins and relations of both family lines.
She was that irreplaceable catalog of relative connections.

When one leaves after lovingly intersecting the lives of so many
A question arises for millennial conversation with the Creator.
Yet there remains for me thankfulness for the serendipitous
Provision of a little sister who will ever be missed—remembered.

Motivation for poem—

Observing my four children, I am always amazed at the bond that exists between them. However, when I think of the bond I had with my own sister, even though she was ten years younger, I guess I shouldn't be so amazed. We have twelve years between our oldest and our youngest. They too have a close bond.

This poem is simply a tribute to my sister, Katherine, an amazing woman with equally amazing giftings. She, for many decades, was the hinge pin for both sides of our family. The apple of her mother's, father's and brother's eye.

GOD'S PROVISION FOR POETIC EXPRESSION

Life events of intense, traumatic impact—
Is it only from these emotional depths
That the poetic juices ooze?
Or can a man without deep emotional tatters
Praise God in a way that truly matters?

What is the source of poetic expression?
Is it from the viscera, the mind or the emotions?
My premise may offer a new revelation.
Not mind, will or emotions—the soul's definition,
Nor visceral depths can meet the poet's ambition.

There is yet to consider that better part—
Not the one often nurtured in the womb
But the one given man before earth's creation.
A third part—Created as Creator is also triune—
From one's personal human spirit can flow that poetic perfume.

Like the Father, man too is three parts:
Spirit, soul and body he is created.
But a man's human spirit is so often in slumber.
It lay asleep, entombed by mind's dominance,
Awaiting restoration to its intended prominence.

Once Divine order is properly re-established—
Triune relation restored to God's original plan,
The poet can dip deep into that bottomless well,
His human spirit—the eternal source for poetic inspiration,
Father's provision from before the dawn of creation.

Motivation for poem—

The impression for this poem came as I was listening to a commentary by the author, John Lithgow. He has published a collection of poems of famous English-speaking poets entitled, *Poets' Corner.* Lithgow presents an interesting profile of each poet's life. I was struck by the common thread of struggles experienced: tragedy, childhood trauma, psychotic bouts, and addictions to name a few.

My question is, could I, or anyone, who has not experienced emotional cataclysm ever adequately express deep thought in vibrant poetic form? Fortunately, my wife has gained revelation of the often overlooked personal, human spirit—"our deeper self." Her textual reference is I Thessalonians 5:23.

Our shared understanding of this verse has been a significant step in the intimacy of our spiritual relationship with Father and with each other.

Oh, yes, as to the question—it may be open to debate, but I believe with an activated and nurtured personal, human spirit one is better equipped to express his heart in poetic form to Father (and possibly to others who might read his work).

THE CURE

Shake; don't stir—
The James Bond cure—
Made every martini a 10.

But now we find
Life's not so sublime
It's simply not that easy.

Though alcohol's great
It's proved quite over rate.
Most problems it does not resolve.

It's through ardent, earnest prayer—
Putting everything in God's care—
Life's crooked path is made straight.

Whether stirred or shaken
When knees are set quakin'
There's that promise from above:

"I'll never leave nor forsake
Even when life's events shake."
On that I can rely.

Motivation for poem—

This poem is not one of my more intellectually demanding ones. The message is pretty straight forward. Unfortunately it is easier written than practiced.

God's promises are the perfect solution to every trial and care of life.

Note to self: believe and practice which you've written.

November 11, 2016

OWNING UP

THE CHALLENGES OF CYBER LAND

My email said—
"Here's a handy pre-populated Tweet."
I could communicate without even a thought.
But it somehow seems like a cyber cheat—
When someone else's words I merely repeat.
Will the reader know it's by another they're taught?

Yes, the repost is by agreement, it's true,
But is it not robbed of creative energy?
No strength of black and white—only a gray hue.
Words of another lose their creative glue—
When separated from conviction's synergy.

"Share," a somewhat similar Facebook action
Repost that friend's poster, picture or request.
One click activates with little thought or exaction.
Quite often no communicated reason—no reaction.
Please, before sharing—add a slice of cerebric zest!

In these times of epic scientific plagiarism
It's no wonder lessons from childhood learned—
Those shades of gray become our baptism.
Resulting today in an author's integrity schism.
For not "owning up" we must be concerned.

Motivation for poem—

Facebook and other social media seem to have evolved into sharing someone's posts—hence someone else's views rather than authoring our own thoughts.

I fear that texting and social media are destroying the beauty and enjoyment of face-to-face verbal communication. I find that even in many personal interactive situations a good bit of my conversation revolves around a "share" that I just read.

Maybe even my experience with Father is becoming more of a "share" relationship rather than a true emotional experience.

February 18, 2016

CAN YOU CALL ME COUNTRY?

I live in the Hills of Tennessee
Do drink wine but I don't smoke—
To some that ain't country—
That's a joke.

I love my wife and my brown dog
Even love to drive my old CJ-5.
Maybe that ain't country,
But I sure do feel alive.

The air is clean, the water pure—
If drinkin' whiskey or sleepin' round
Is what it takes to be country crowned—
Then don't call me country.

Call me what you will—
Just let me live,
Then when I die—
Bury me here
On my Tennessee hill.

Motivation for poem—

The Dolly Parton fund raiser for the forest fire devastation in Sevier County, Tennessee, featured one country music performer after another.

    The lyrics sung by some afforded a whole different picture of country than to what I care to plead. About two hours into the show, the definitional dichotomy of "country" began to take poetic form.

    I fully realize I share a great many of the values of being country and yet would not want to be credited with others.

    The question remains then, how does one measure his country quotient? I have a feeling there may not be a standard by which to measure. There are degrees of country depending upon the *self-evaluation* of the observer—the more country I consider myself, the higher the definitional bar of country.

    As the poem says, regardless of how an observer sees me, I love the Tennessee hills and adopt much of the country lifestyle.

    May my bones go back to dust in the embrace of those hills.

December 13, 2016

CHAPTER FOUR

Eclectic continued, but more spiritual in content

Gentle breath stirs trees—
As leaves make their hushed rustle.
Will some fall earthward?

THE SHINING PATH

Much of life is like the shining path
That seems to light my way
Across the forest floor.

When aimlessly followed
My unknown destination will have
No reward.

Discernment must govern
The path I choose.

I ask divine guidance
On each path's beckoning way.

On this true source of direction
I can rely.

Let Father alone guide me
Through the wilderness of life.

With every beckoning, shining path
I must determine first if it is His glow.

Motivation for poem—

First, let me say, the haiku introducing this chapter has a metaphoric quality. I trust Holy Spirit stirs my spirit and from that stirring some poetic leaves may fall.

Now, about this poem—my first recalled experience of seeing a shining path in the woods came while seeking my way through a forest in Kwa-Zulu Natal, South Africa.

This was some 20 years ago, but the memory is vivid and has often replayed. I was seeing what appeared to be a well-worn path shining ahead of me. The leaves on the ground fairly glowed, seeming to clearly present a path.

I followed the path some distance before an inner compass said it could not be right. Each direction I turned another path seemed to light up. I cannot scientifically explain the phenomenon, but it was real.

As I said, I have witnessed it many times since—even again today during a walk through my Tennessee woods.

Because of this experience I could not resist writing a poem. Especially since this date celebrates nearly a year of release of poetic spirit.

December 12, 2016

TRUE NORTH

There lies somewhere in the polar north
An enormous mother lode—
With unerring accuracy it draws the compass needle
To its hidden depths.

How much like sin this deception speaks
Luring each to rely on an off-course life
Till at the end, when destination reached,
No time for correction remains.

For most of life, magnetic north will get one by—
But the wise traveler will stay a true heading,
Always making correction to keep true north—
Even when life's storms would blow off track.

Come 'round to that North Star's unerring path—
Make correction against that subtle deception—
Resist its magnetic attraction.
Let no other choice alter your path from True North.

Motivation for poem—

While on the theme of guidance and direction, let's look at the poem *True North*.

I so appreciated a recent, thought-provoking Facebook post. Many valid points were made, along with the reference to true north being reflected by the compass. The metaphor was used to show that being one degree off wouldn't get you to your destination—true.

However, in my old Boy Scout days, some 70 years ago, I learned about "magnetic declination." This was the correction that had to be made from magnetic north of a compass to true north. So, for me, the metaphor didn't ring true.

As I continued to think about the compass deception—the metaphor of magnetic north being like sin came to me. The subtly of sin can lead you throughout life just slightly off course, *even if you know the truth.* How sad to end my life's journey, only to find I was following the wrong guidance.

As we travel through life there are many adjustments of choice that we must be aware of and make. We know life's destination: to arrive at True North. How special to think Yeshua is that infallible, guiding North Star.

January 8, 2017

NAGGING MEMORY OF
A FADED DREAM

As night escapes pursued by morning's light
Those things dark are now made bright.
The night's dream, its reality drained,
Nags still to be explained.

Was there purpose that should now appear,
If hazy recollection were made clear?
That face and those words spoken
In day's light only a memory broken.

Relationships now viewed from afar
By the light of day seem so bizarre.
Those words spoken, however, reveal
Emotions hidden—
Now through dream—vented with zeal.

Perhaps the therapist would wisely explain:
"You're being given a chance to deal with pain.
Don't disregard that nagging recollection–
Take a moment for a bit of earnest introspection."

An ardent prayer should be timely offered:
"Take me where those hurtful words were proffered.
What's the source of that nocturnal vent?
I desire to set straight, annul—yes, repent."

Vows and judgments uttered from earliest days—
Those words and thoughts contrary to love's ways
Are like those seeds when into the ground are sown
Bear fruit according to their kind—full grown.

The blood of Yeshua remains the answer
To wash what Spirit reveals is "cancer".
That dream-stirred memory will be a blessing
When love's past failings receive
blood washed confessing.

Motivation for poem—

Dreams have been the subject of many prayer sessions over the sixty plus years of our marriage. I am a prolific dreamer. My dreams have ranged from seemingly nonsensical to profoundly prophetic.

In the 1980s, we learned from the writing of John and Paula Sandford the power of our judgments and vows—even those expressed in our most formative years. The "hurtful words" mentioned in this poem could arise from a judgment or vow I had made as a youth, but manifest now in the present.

Our dream state is a fertile ground for revelation of emotional trauma. During sleep the control over the conscious mind is relaxed and our human spirit can orchestrate the dialogue. The Scripture says that he whom the Son sets free is free indeed. (John 8:31-36) This promise establishes prerequisites: abiding and knowing. God's teachers have been given revelation for effectively accessing these promises.

The prayer the poem suggests is for the "source and origin" of the troubling dream scenario. The authority for this request is part of the "abiding and knowing" expressed in John. Our introduction to this prayer protocol came from the teaching of Dr. Ed Smith, Transformation Ministry (originally Theophostic Prayer).

As the poem concludes, it is not the wisdom of man which effects healing and change, it is the blood of Yeshua applied to the revealed, locked away memory.

March 13, 2016

DREAMS AND VISIONS
BRING HEALING

An event so firmly, indelibly writ—
The memory like an unhealed sore
Leaves my soul deep cut and rend;
No solace seemingly to be found.

When all things are made new
This darkness must loose.
That hurt—its glue so firmly fixed,
No longer casts its shadow from the past.

Standing then in the light of God's own Son
All past wounds will be forever healed,
But must I wait 'til then for absolution?
What in the present will erase my memory's wound?

Now as sleep steals o'er that memory's face,
Must my question await the morning's light?
Perhaps dreams and visions give answers.
Slumber nears—prayer fades—my spirit remains ascended
to His holy presence.

During the night, before first light—came the number "seven."
Can a number heal what my memory won't release?
Perhaps the number contains some mystic explanation.
The night is not over—answers may yet be revealed.

Questioning thoughts come: must that hurtful memory by definition be bad?
Even though distasteful, could there be a redemptive purpose?
And that number seven—are ancient roots its secret message?
Before I wake will my lamp of understanding be lit?

When a memory shouts a condemning refrain—
If that scenario has already been blood-washed,
Can that memory come again with condemnation?
Perhaps an unhealed soul dominates my spirit's faith.

My human spirit must be liberated to discern that incessant voice—
Does the message destroy or does it restore—which has love its source?
My last sleep-muffled question: And what of that number seven?
Perhaps His Word holds the key for meaningful understanding.

Sabbath, two feasts and Naaman's healing,
Jericho and Aaron's consecration—all by seven linked.
These six events share one common explanation—
Obedience—but to what discipline am I called?

How is this seeming continued condemnation linked to obedience?
I hear: "If you are the Son of God—come down off that cross."
Then the divine response: "Forgive them Father, they know not...."
Obedience and intercession punctuated by the Roman spike.

The night's conclusion: when a painful, accusing memory calls—
Knowledge of blood-bought forgiveness summons Intercession.
Not for me, but for those caught in the trap I've escaped.
The memory now becomes a redemptive trigger, no more a devastating voice.

Motivation for poem—

I wrote this poem while I was in the midst of the seven-day observance of The Feast of Unleavened Bread. Each day I would offer to the Lord my life's leaven. On this particular day an old, recurring memory tinged with condemnation came to mind. The original event which caused me emotional trauma was not of my doing. I did not know of it until years after it had occurred. I always felt the sting of condemnation whenever the memory surfaced because of ignorance of the event—my failure to be a spiritual covering for my family. I knew I had been forgiven by all involved and that the sin was "under the blood." Yet, that barb of guilt and failure remained.

I submitted the recalled event to the Lord, placing the scenario on the altar in the tabernacle in my heart. As I laid this pain before Him, I heard the number "seven". I did eventually come to understand that where I had once felt condemnation it was now an opportunity for intercession.

Did I hear the number "seven" because of the seven-day Feast I was observing? I don't know, but faithful Yahovah used many parts to put together a cognitive whole. I no longer fear triggers to that memory. Rather I now almost joyfully anticipate an opportunity to intercede as He leads. What a beautiful experience of Yahovah's redemptive healing power.

April 3, 2016

SACRIFICE PONDERED

Sacrifice . . . not a pleasant word:
Conjuring up thoughts of pain
A surrender of possessions to gain favor
An offering given out of fear or force.

What if that is not a definition properly perceived,
But came from a lexicon of ancient pagan practice,
At the altars of gods of stone and wood, devoid of heart.
What if the Chosen's alien experience
Muddled their discerning aright God's intent?

For now, look away from this speculation—
Instead, what does history record?
Was our creation like the voodoo doll
Made for vexing with pins and incantation?
Or, was is not the Divine plan to have an intimate relation?

"Make man in our image," the call for man's creation—
When Spirit-breathed, man was given life—
Intimate garden walks together to be enjoyed—
No linking of punitive sacrifice.

The first recorded sacrificial offering was made,
Not by demand, but from hearts of thankfulness.
Perhaps it was then that the heart's condition
Became the gold standard test—
And Cain fell short of giving the very best.

That word "sacrifice" when generationally traced,
If Yahovah is involved, is never meant for punishment.
So perhaps the word's Hebrew translation to English does
not communicate its truth—
But it too is tainted more by pagan root.

When at Sinai's base the Chosen declined
That indwelling intimacy offered by Father,
The specter of sacrifice in the fire's golden glow
Began to define and satisfy intimacy's hunger.

The Creator seeking to stir the hearts of His created
Proclaimed that He would dwell—
not as He wanted,
But in constructed splendor; now with human intercession—
Prescribed rituals defining the Divine relation.

Millennia then spent, with and without God's earthly abode—
Awaiting Messiah's prophesied restoration of intimacy lost—
This time from Zion's mount.

But for believers in Messiah Yeshua,
The Bridegroom's presence has
For millennia been offered with blood-bought cost.
The promise of His indwelling so freely given.

All thoughts of sacrifice having lost its pagan definition—
Replaced by an intimacy restored and wrapped in love—
Return of thankfulness for His indwelling presence.
The hunger that would cry out for pagan sacrifice forever quelled.

Motivation for poem—

Most of us don't like to think we are called to sacrifice. Perhaps the word has been abused in its definition or in the reason for institution of the idea.

It seems God never asked for sacrifices in the beginning—they were voluntarily offered as thanksgiving and honoring of Yahweh.

When the people at Sinai opted for Moses to represent them before Yahweh, the sacrificial system came into being. They rejected a personal relationship so God had to establish a substitute menu of what would please and honor Him.

I believe the effort required to meet a standard of praise and honor became part of this system of sacrifice. Maybe it was a little reminder of what the relationship might have been as through, Yeshua, it would become.

THE CONSEQUENCE OF
CEREBRAL DEMISE

HOW FINAL IS DEATH'S DESTRUCTION?

Let us consider that cerebral hard drive
On which is recorded our every thought and deed.
It is truly a wonder while we are alive–
But what happens should that faculty no longer thrive?
Yes, what happens when it's an update we need?

Is that data, so faithfully recorded, now lost?
Each thought, each deed whatever the price,
Is no longer on that hard drive faithfully embossed?
These records are on history's ash heap tossed?
To some that prospect of death's finality is oh so nice.

All of life's failures and faults gone through demise–
Yes, to some a most comforting provision.
But perhaps we should not be too quick to surmise–
All is gone, all erased–no need for disguise.
There is One who does not share this vision.

Did you ever hear of the Lamb's Book of Life?
Best authority tells us such a book is written.
The ultimate eternal backup–where is recorded–every single strife—
From womb to grave each thought, each deed of life–
No comfort found there for any sin by His blood not smitten.

So, cranial miracle of Yahovah's calculation
Your recording apparatus does not with death compromise.
No indeed, so take care—tend to each sin's eradication
The shed blood of Yeshua is offered to all God's creation–
Appropriating leaves no question of cerebral demise.

Motivation for poem—

"Ashes to ashes, dust to dust." Some would like to think that all lifestyle choices will be settled by death. When the brain stops working, are all our deeds, good and bad, really just gone? Will there be no life's accounting required?

Many folks certainly hope so. But for two millennia there have been millions of people who believe otherwise. Unfortunately, it will be too late for those who think cerebral demise cancels the consequences of life's choices.

For me, life is not about whether my choices have post-death consequences; rather, am I faithfully seeking and walking the path Yahovah has for me?

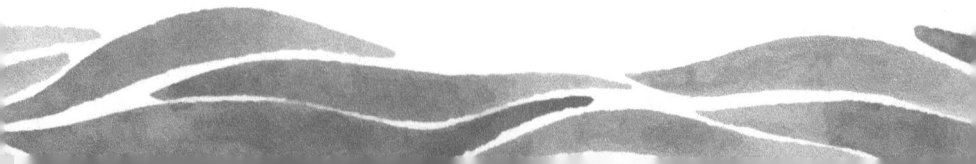

HE FROM HIS GLORY CALLED

At Exodus' close we are plainly told
Yahovah's glory filled the tabernacle.
Through this show of fearsome force
No man could invade the Creator's splendor.

Was this separation Yahovah's final word—
Like the penalty for Adam's unrepented sin—
No more of those cool, evening walks
The garden's intimacy forever to surrender?

Yet was there not that burning bush
From which He spoke with words of passion,
To balance at Sinai's cloud-covered mount
Those displays of force He did engender—

Sinai, where those gathered were held at bay.
But wait! One man stood above the cowering crowd.
One man was called to ascend that mount.
One man was bid God's glory enter.

Can it be that again in Leviticus' record
The mystery resolves itself by divine direction:
The book's name, when in Hebrew spoken, is
Vayikra "and he called"—with voice most tender.

Eden's closed gate was not His heart—
It was the created's heart that stood them apart.
That fearsome reality from Sinai demonstrated
That rejection of intimacy came from the offender.

A substitute offered for His indwelling desire:
A tabernacle built to His heavenly design;
Intimacy now through a priest, an intercessor—
A legal definition for each offering to render.

A second chance from a loving Father to gain this "slavery's" end—
To walk that glorious road to intimacy's freedom.
This time purchased by the shed blood of Father's Son—
The resurrected, promised Messiah who calls from Glory across the ages
the blessing of intimacy gained through surrender.

Motivation for poem—

Once again the Torah provides inspiration for my poetry. In these first five books of the Bible, God often demonstrates His "disgust" with His creation. From Adam's garden deception to the nation Israel gathered by Moses before Mt. Sinai and beyond.

It would appear there is a trail of disbelief, unbelief and rejection by God's chosen of their Creator.

The Tabernacle whose construction is commissioned, designed and then gloriously occupied by God seems to evidence His decision to "distance" Himself from the people, yet maintain a presence. His preference for indwelling was exchanged for the formality of a ritualistic priesthood. It is the people (down to the present age), not God, who continue to resist His desired intimacy.

His "plan" will be ultimately finalized with a last appearance from Yeshua after which all offers of indwelling glory and intimacy will be terminated.

However, I do not want to dwell on the negatives except to point out the overwhelming glory of God that He offers those who accept His invitation. Words can barely hint at the contrast between the options.

THE CLOUD, THE GLORY
AND THE POET

In cloud o'er Sinai's mount Yahovah's presence was revealed,
In like signature with force the tabernacle He sealed.
But 'twas not the vision of cloud alone
That made so clear His very presence known.

When Moses, a proven, mighty man of God,
Could not enter, where before he'd trod.
Because an unseen force did mysteriously operate
Blocking his way—God's manifest presence—a closed gate.

What appropriate word can English give
So that this experience one might relive?
"Glory"—the word translators confidently say
Does that rapturous moment of time convey.

"*Kabowd*" is the word in Hebrew we are told.
Yet that too is lacking in descriptive gold.
To the poet there is simply not *one* word;
Something much deeper must be stirred.

A force so tangible, yet wholly unseen,
Speaks of forces far from routine.
Such a force field we've yet to discover—
A secret not given man's mind to uncover.

Where then does the poet need to turn—
From what source can he possibly learn?
There is but one connection to be found:
Ascend by personal spirit to that heavenly ground.

There in the delight of His love and peace
No hint of the awesome force He could release.
Though words still fail this poet's pen,
To be in that Presence I will return again and again.

Motivation for poem—

Continuing with the theme of the indescribable magnitude of God's manifested glory, I turn again to Torah.

A quandary of how to explain the majesty described in Parsha *P'kudei* (Ex 38:21-40:38)

> *Then the cloud covered the tabernacle of meeting, and the glory of the Lord filled the tabernacle. And Moses was not able to enter the tabernacle of meeting, because the cloud rested above it, and the glory of the Lord filled the tabernacle.*—Exodus 40:34-35

The word "glory" seems so inadequate to explain that daunting, manifested presence of Yahweh into which Moses could not enter. A descriptive challenge to communicate whether in prose or poetry.

CHAPTER FIVE

Haiku philosophy

While yet in my bed
On dreary, rainy morning
Haiku brightens day.

Motivation for the haiku—

I think of the haiku as a glimpsed thought or observation succinctly expressed.

There are different schools of proper haiku expression, but I prefer the simple scheme of 5-7-5: five syllables in the first line, seven in the second and a repeat of five in the third and final line.

I will certainly not provide a motivation for each haiku submitted—most are fairly expressive of the circumstance giving rise to the verse.

Because of the 5-7-5 restraint it is fun to be challenged by the legalism of this form of expression.

I call this chapter *haiku philosophy.* It is often the very succinctness of the form that excites the reader's imagination to understand what philosophical depth has impressed the author.

Enjoy!

SIX HAIKU OF NATURE

A varied green wall
Greets my sleepy eyes at dawn—
Trees in their spring dress.

~

Leaden sky at morn
Precipitation's gray form.
Wet earth will return.

~

Shadows slowly creep
Down driveway's quiet, stony path.
Sun makes its orbit.

~

Gentle breath stirs trees
As leaves make their hushed rustle—
Will some fall earthward?

~

Sun shines through window.
Morning light cast long shadow.
Noon will shorten it.

~

An ant bit my foot—
Totally audacious act.
Can he hope to win?

SIX HAIKU FROM THE FARM

The donkeys are gone—
Neither missed nor lamented.
What will replace them?

~

Drove to the mailbox.
Nice run for my dog River.
Big day at the farm.

~

Two old women sit—
Gazing at the gloomy day.
What will bring them joy?
(not one of my wife's favorites)

~

My wife has many hats—
Each she wears so very well.
I am that witness.

~

Two donkeys are gone.
Three sheep graze as replacement.
Better days ahead?

~

Some days no haiku.
Events are not that way bent.
So this Thursday went.

A HAIKU DIALOGUE

A Facebook post exchange:

Chickens failed again!
Rule—no Sabbath egg laying.
They ignored the day.

~

Wife's suggestion:

"No Sabbath egg laying."
Six hens ignored Sabbath rule.
They laid anyway.

~

Daughter, Christina, suggested egg laying is not work, only a "bodily function"—my reply:

Daughter's wisdom boggles:
"Bodily function is not work!"
Chickens are off hook!

CONCLUDING FIVE HAIKU OF TOMFOOLERY

Clever fellow he
Who understands haikueze—
Like falling off log.

~

TV's muted voice.
AC's background hum drones on.
Doctor's office wait.

~

Computer software—
Bugs no spray will ever reach.
Brain frazzled trying.

~

My children are grown.
The youngest now forty four—
No longer blank slates.

~

Digitization.
One word, yet first Haiku verse.
Poets say not fair.

CHAPTER SIX

Poetic reflection on miracles

His creative force
Foiling Satan's every plan
God's mighty power.

Motivation for poem—

I have chosen to devote the last chapter solely to one rather short poem. However, the subject of God's creative power in conjunction with healing is to me so profound I wanted to leave the reader with a challenging spiritual premise to consider.

In the first Torah teaching for Genesis it speaks of God creating *out of nonexistence* all of the manifestations of creation—He spoke *nothing* into being.

The gospel of John in Chapter 1 tells us that nothing came into being except through Yeshua, that is, the unified God.

I have summarized this for my understanding by saying that everything we physically experience is the product of the manifesting of the laws of God.

Disease, in my understanding then, is not a product of Satan— he has no creative power. Disease is the resultant product of God's laws of creation. Unfortunately, because of sin, Satan can manipulate these laws to work to man's detriment. On the other hand God has created man with capacity to study and understand His laws of creative force. This understanding can be for man's good—hence healthy diet, exercise, mental health, even pharmaceuticals are an application of God's laws resulting in our good.

Further, I believe God is pleased when man ponders and understands the application of His laws in obtaining physical and emotional good fruit as well as avoiding bad fruit.

As an example, I believe He delights when man can find what application of His law produces a particular disease—bad fruit.

As we all know man continues to run up against manifestations of the law in diseases which defy understanding. It is at these times that the default solution can only be the "miracle." And really, what is the miracle, except requesting God to undue the law that He knows is being applied, but which man hasn't discovered. In other words, we are asking Him to *return to nonexistence the thing that vexes us.* Hence, the grist for this poem.

November 24, 2016

GOD'S CREATIVE POWER

The creative power of God:
From *nothing* everything came forth.

The creative power of man
Involves starting from *something* in every plan.

Man works to heal what is—
Within the laws of Divine creation
He seeks solutions for disease cessation.

When faced with problems
Which have no known reconciliation
Man must then ask God to return to its nonexistence
This impossible vexation!

Epilogue to poem

If Yeshua has been given all power, which He has—He is God come in the flesh, then what is it we ask in His name? Are we not in those cases of seeming incurable emotional or physical disability believing that the power of the created condition will be removed; that it might be returned to a state of nonexistence. I hope this understanding changes the intercessory prayers of the believer.

GLOSSARY

PARSHA, PARSHAT, PARSHAH. All different English spellings of the same Hebrew word meaning part or portion. Refers to the weekly reading of a portion of the Torah. These portions have been established for centuries in Judaism and their study is embraced by most Messianic believers as a weekly spiritual/devotional exercise.

SHABBAT. The Hebrew word for Sabbath, the seventh day of the week called Saturday on the Justinian calendar. It is not a day of man's choosing, but God's.

TORAH. The first five books of the Old Testament. Also commonly used to mean the law. A better definition incorporates the idea of instruction, guidance. It is more than just the law and commandments for we can take guidance from the opening words of Genesis to the end of Deuteronomy.

YAHWEH AND YAHOVAH are English created words for the Hebrew scripture name of God, yhvh (yod hey vav hey) In Judaism the name of God is arbitrarily written as Adonai even though it has the English equivalent spelling of yhvh. This is because of the holiness of the name. Conservative Judaism even omits the 'o' when writing the name God, instead writing G-d. Adonai (yhvh) is generally translated in English Bibles as *Lord*. I have used both Yahweh and Yahovah. In later writing I have leaned toward Yahovah as it seems closer to yhvh.

YESHUA. The Hebrew name Jesus' mother would have used with him. From Yehoshua/Yeshua – Jesus' name in Hebrew – we get the Greek transliteration Iesous, which was transliterated into Latin as Iesus and later became the English name, Jesus. (JewishVoice.org)